Amazing Young People

RUBY BRIDGES

Martha London

DiscoverRoo
An Imprint of Pop!
popbooksonline.com

abdobooks.com

Published by Pop!, a division of ABDO, PO Box 398166, Minneapolis, Minnesota 55439.

Printed in China

052019
092019

THIS BOOK CONTAINS RECYCLED MATERIALS

Cover Photo: Paul Slade/Paris Match Archive/Getty Images

Interior Photos: Paul Slade/Paris Match Archive/Getty Images, 1, 11, 12, 15; AP Images, 5, 14, 17, 21, 22 (right), 25; iStockphoto, 6, 13, 20, 23 (bottom), 29, 30, 31; Red Line Editorial, 7; Don Cravens/The LIFE Images Collection/Getty Images, 8; Dennis Van Tine/Abaca/Abacapress.com/Newscom, 9; PA/AP Images, 18; Lane Turner/The Boston Globe/Getty Images, 19; Shutterstock Images, 22 (left); Suzanne Plunkett/AP Images, 23 (top); Album/Fine Art Images/Newscom, 26–27; Tina Fineberg/AP Images, 28

Editor: Brienna Rossiter
Series Designer: Sarah Taplin

Library of Congress Control Number: 2018964788

Publisher's Cataloging-in-Publication Data

Names: London, Martha, author.

Title: Ruby Bridges / by Martha London.

Description: Minneapolis, Minnesota : Pop!, 2020 | Series: Amazing young people | Includes online resources and index.

Identifiers: ISBN 9781532163692 (lib. bdg.) | ISBN 9781644940426 (pbk.) | ISBN 9781532165139 (ebook)

Subjects: LCSH: Bridges, Ruby--Juvenile literature. | Civil rights activists--Biography--Juvenile literature. | School integration--United States--Juvenile literature. | Desegregation--Juvenile literature.

Classification: DDC 370.193 [B]--dc23

WELCOME TO DiscoverRoo!

Pop open this book and you'll find QR codes loaded with information, so you can learn even more!

Scan this code* and others like it while you read, or visit the website below to make this book pop!

popbooksonline.com/ruby-bridges

*Scanning QR codes requires a web-enabled smart device with a QR code reader app and a camera.

TABLE OF CONTENTS

CHAPTER 1
SEPARATE SCHOOLS

Ruby Bridges was part of the **civil rights movement**. She grew up in Louisiana during the 1950s and 1960s. At that time, many towns in the United States were **segregated**. Laws

WATCH A VIDEO HERE!

Students attend a segregated school in Rockmart, Georgia, in 1950.

kept black people and white people apart. They went to separate schools, restaurants, and stores.

In 1954, segregation in schools became illegal. But many schools did not follow this new rule. They continued to accept only white students. Black children had to go to separate schools. These schools received less money. They couldn't offer students as many classes or opportunities.

Many schools for black students struggled to pay for teachers and supplies.

SCHOOLS IN 1964

Ten years after segregation became illegal, some schools remained segregated in these states.

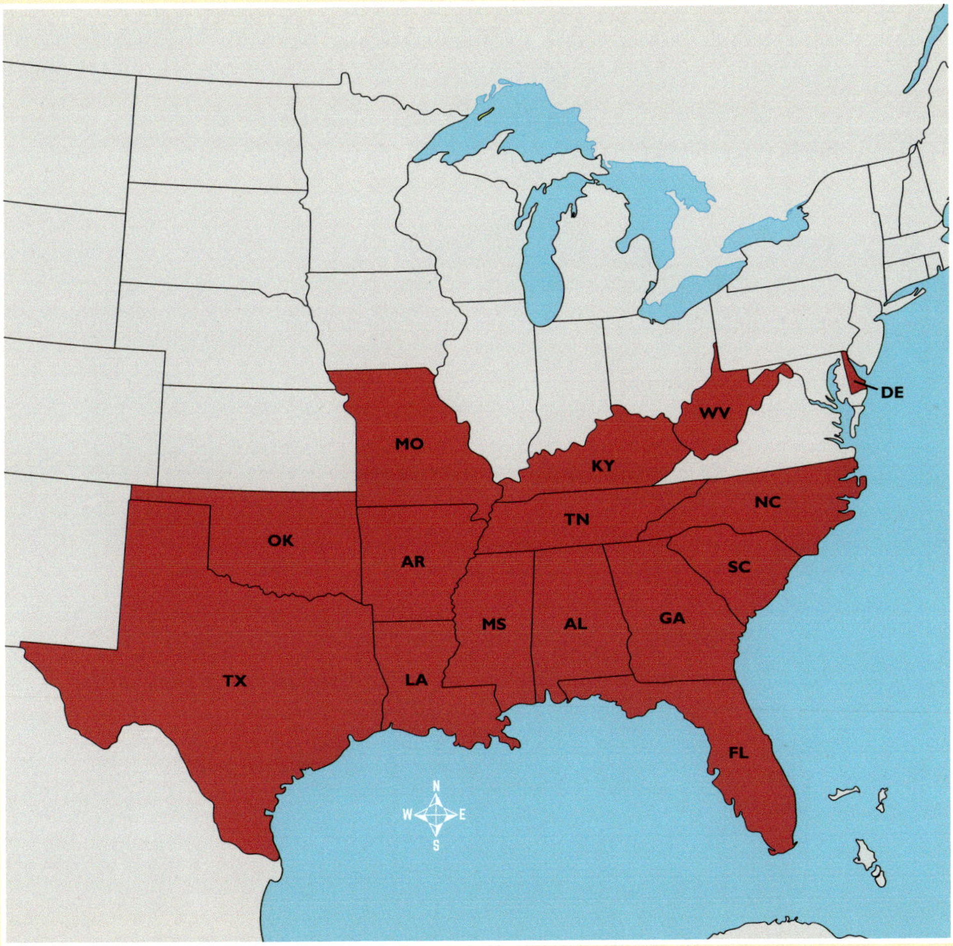

In 1959, a judge said Louisiana schools had to **integrate**. The next year, Ruby became the first black student to attend William Frantz Elementary

Unlike many judges in the South, Judge J. Skelly Wright supported integration.

Today, Ruby continues using education to fight racism.

School. She was only six years old. But she helped black students gain equal education.

DID YOU KNOW?

Some schools closed so they wouldn't have to accept black students.

CHAPTER 2

A RIGHT TO LEARN

Ruby Bridges was born on September 8, 1954. Her family moved to New Orleans, Louisiana, when she was four years old. Her parents wanted her to get a good education.

LEARN MORE HERE!

Ruby studies with her father, Abon, and her mother, Lucille.

DID YOU KNOW?

Ruby's father worked at a gas station. Her mother took care of Ruby and her siblings.

Ruby plays with a group of friends.

Ruby went to a **segregated** school for kindergarten. Then, in 1960, New Orleans created a test for black students. If students passed, they could go to **integrated** schools. The schools hoped the students would fail. But six black students passed, including Ruby. She planned to attend William Frantz in the fall.

DID YOU KNOW?

Three of the other students went to a different all-white school. The other two stayed at their old schools.

Some people held signs outside the school.

The school tried to stop Ruby from attending. So did many white families whose children went there. Some parents pulled their kids out of school.

Others threatened to hurt Ruby.

Families who didn't want to integrate held classes at a factory instead.

CHAPTER 3

INTEGRATION BEGINS

Ruby's first day at William Frantz Elementary was November 14, 1960. The US government sent **marshals** to keep her safe. Even so, large crowds gathered outside the school. Ruby had to walk

COMPLETE AN ACTIVITY HERE!

US marshals walked with Ruby to and from school each day.

past them to go to class. Some people yelled at her. Others threw things.

Some parents tried to stop other families from attending.

Angry parents came to take their kids out of school. It was not safe for Ruby to attend class. She spent the day

Barbara Henry holds a photo of herself and Ruby in the classroom.

in the principal's office. After that, Ruby was in a class by herself.

BARBARA HENRY

Barbara Henry was Ruby's first-grade teacher. The other teachers refused to have Ruby in their classes. But Barbara worked hard to help and protect Ruby. Over the year, they became close. Barbara often sat at a desk right beside Ruby. Sometimes they ate lunch together too.

Ruby and her teacher spent all day in the classroom. Ruby couldn't eat lunch with the other students. She couldn't

Ruby often had her lessons on the chalkboard near the front of the class.

Police officers had to stay outside the school.

play with them either. And each day, she had to walk past the angry crowd.

DID YOU KNOW?

The rest of Ruby's family also faced challenges. Her father lost his job.

TIMELINE

1954
Ruby Bridges is born in Mississippi on September 8.

1958
Ruby's family moves to New Orleans, Louisiana.

1960
Ruby begins attending first grade at William Frantz Elementary School.

1972
Ruby graduates from Francis T. Nicholls High School.

1984
Ruby marries Malcolm Hall.

1999
Ruby forms the Ruby Bridges Foundation.

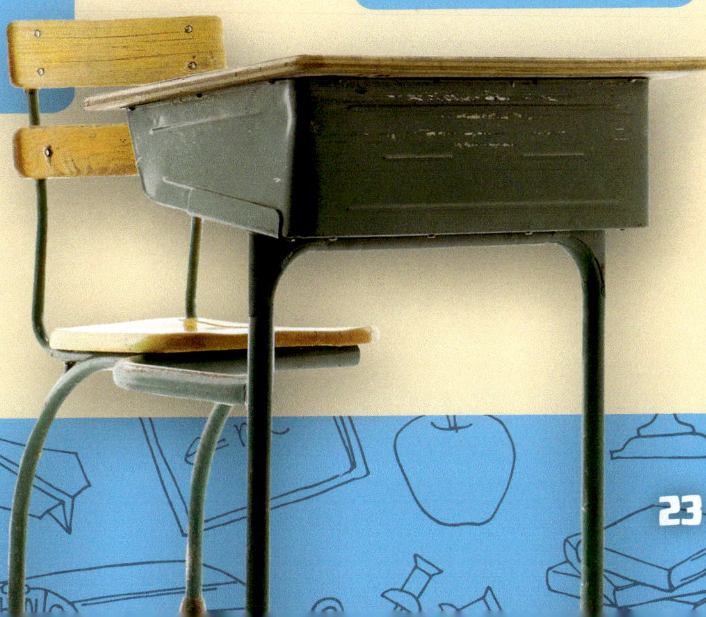

CHAPTER 4

MAKING CHANGES

Ruby's year at William Frantz was not easy. She was often lonely and scared. But she kept going to school. Gradually, other students returned to the school. Ruby even met some of them.

LEARN MORE HERE!

By December, several of the white children who had left William Frantz were attending classes again.

The next year, Ruby was in a class with other students. She no longer needed **marshals** to guard her. Other

Norman Rockwell painted a famous picture of Ruby called **The Problem We All Live With.**

black students began attending the school. And in 1972, Ruby graduated from an **integrated** high school.

Ruby reads a book about her life to first graders at a school in New York in 2000.

As an adult, Ruby continued to work for **racial equality**. She focused on schools and education. In 1999, she created the Ruby Bridges **Foundation**.

The Ruby Bridges Foundation helps students learn to treat one another with respect.

This group works to help all people be treated equally and fairly.

DID YOU KNOW?

After high school, Ruby went to business school. Then she got a job as a travel agent.

MAKING CONNECTIONS

TEXT-TO-SELF

When have you kept doing something, even when it was hard? What made you choose to keep trying?

TEXT-TO-TEXT

Have you read other books about people who worked to end segregation? How were their actions similar to or different from Ruby's?

TEXT-TO-WORLD

Ruby's parents believed education was important. What is something you value? How does that shape your actions?

GLOSSARY

civil rights movement – a struggle in the 1950s and 1960s that involved people working to gain equal rights for black people.

foundation – an organization that gives money to support a cause or make change.

integrate – to bring people together rather than separating them.

marshal – a law enforcement officer who works for the US government.

racial equality – giving equal rights and opportunities to all people, regardless of their race.

segregate – to separate people based on the color of their skin.

INDEX

ONLINE RESOURCES

popbooksonline.com

Scan this code* and others like it while you read, or visit the website below to make this book pop!

popbooksonline.com/ruby-bridges

*Scanning QR codes requires a web-enabled smart device with a QR code reader app and a camera.